MAP OF GHANA

Ghana is located in West Africa, 8° north of the Equator and 2° west of the Prime Meridian. It is bordered by the Gulf of Guinea and Atlantic Ocean to the south; Cote D'Ivoire to the west; Burkina Faso to the north; and Togo to the east. The total area is 239,460 sq. km; of which 230,940 sq. km is land; and 8,520 sq. km is water.

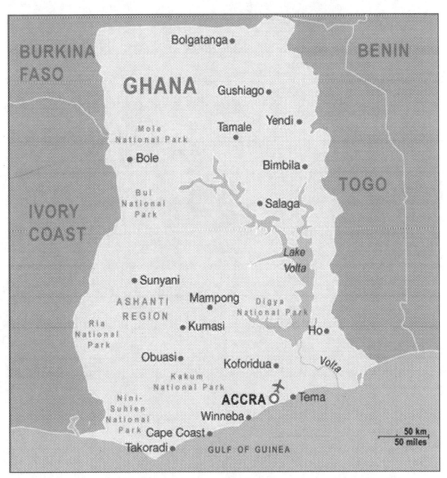

Map courtesy of www.theodora.com/maps, used with permission.

The Map of Africa

HEY,
YOU BETTER
KNOW
BEFORE
YOU GO!

D. N. A.

Order this book online at www.trafford.com
or email orders@trafford.com

Most Trafford titles are also available at major online book retailers.

1st copyright and print by DNA was 1998 Revised 1999
Reprinted 2004

Printed in the United States of America.

ISBN: 978-1-4269-9602-3 (sc)
ISBN: 978-1-4269-9603-0 (e)

First Edition

Published by iTAL™ Kingsway Publications, International

Montego Bay, Jamaica West Indies

Detroit, Michigan

Ghana, West Africa

Library of Congress Control Number 200911756

Also by D. N. A. **iTALWAY™ HANDBOOK: Medicine Plants and Home Remedies**

Trafford rev. 10/31/2011

   www.trafford.com

North America & international
toll-free: 1 888 232 4444 (USA & Canada)
phone: 250 383 6864 ♦ fax: 812 355 4082

CONTENTS

SINCERE THANKS FROM DJENABA

My deepest thanks to the Heavenly Mother / Father for blessing me with a husband, parents, family and beloved friends for their eternal love and support. I extend a special thank you to all who purchase my travel book. My publication is a general handbook applicable for travels throughout the Motherland. Give Thanks.

∞

E-Books available via: The Shrines of the Black Madonna Culture Center and Bookstore—Houston, TX, Atlanta, GA or Detroit, MI; Truth Bookstore Southfield, MI; Barnes and Noble; Baker and Taylor; Amazon—Kindle; Google; and Kindle for IPhone

FOREWORD

I've always had a 'hankerin' to travel and write.

For those who have heard the call of our Ancestral Homeland and have longed to make the journey forward, may these helpful tips better prepare you for the return to the Motherland—Africa. After living in Jamaica for many years, I have been properly indoctrinated for life in Africa. In fact, Jamaica is a twin/'atta', nation to Ghana, but on a much smaller scale. The agriculture, woodlands, resources, aquatic life, geography, self-enterprising hawkers/vendors, push/pull carts, cultural craft industry, artisans, manual labor vs. machinery, and the multitude of natural resources looked s-o-o-o familiar! It seemed like I was still in the West Indies; except, Jamaica's tranquil blue sea had been replaced by the raging ancestral, spiritual waters of the **African Holocaust**, the Gulf of Guinea. (B. K. A. the trans-Atlantic European Slave Trade).

My first visit to Ghana was a ten day tour in 1998, as part of the Jamaican Emancipation Delegation, which brought the ancestral remains from 'Jahland' to Ghana's 1st Emancipation Celebration.

In 1999, I bought a one-way ticket to Africa, shipped my work equipment, personal effects, and a vehicle (that was quite an ordeal and extremely costly) to Ghana. I knew I was home—

BACKGROUND OF GHANA

Ghana, formerly The Ghana Empire, The Gold Coast, The Republic of Ghana, was the first African country to be liberated from the United Kingdom on March 6, 1957. Kwame Nkrumah was appointed as the first President by the Big Five. Ghana endured a long series of coups before Flight Lt. Jerry Rawlings, our relative, took power in 1981. "President Rawlings promptly banned all political parties. After approving a new constitution and restoring multiparty politics in 1992, J. J. Rawlings won the presidential elections in 1992 and 1996, but was constitutionally prevented from running for a third term in 2000. John Kufuor succeeded him and was reelected in 2004. John Atta Mills was elected as head of state in early 2009." [The World Factbook, 2009]

Ghana, a tropical, peaceful, Democratic Society, has been visited by three U. S. Presidents—Carter, Bush and Barack Obama. English and a multitude of dialects are spoken throughout the ten, (10) regions: Accra, Ashanti, Brong-Ahafo, Central, Eastern, Greater Northern, Upper East, Upper West, Volta, and Western.

Are you able to read weights, distance, measurements and temperatures in METRIC? **Hey, you better know before you go!** Start sharpening your conversion skills because Ghana uses the metric system—exclusively. Akwaaba, welcome to Ghana, a member of ECOWAS—**E**conomic **C**ommunities **O**f **W**est **A**frican **S**tates.

PRIOR TO DEPARTURE

Six (6) months prior to departure, go to the library or browse the internet of your intended destination to familiarize yourself with the following suggestions, which are applicable to every country in Africa.

> Geography
> Climate
> Culture
> Agriculture
> Religion
> Language
> Philosophy
> Government
> Tourist sites
> Foreign exchange rates

Utilize a reputable source for up-to-date information about safe hotels, access to ATM machines, ground transportation, pre-paid international cell phone accounts, roaming fees and other points of concerns from your local provider. Notify your credit card company that you intend to travel abroad, so that your future charges and debits made in Ghana will be authorized.

Certain U.S. cell phone companies offer international roaming, at cost, if you decide to take your U.S. cell. Contact your cell provider for details. Two economical alternatives: buy a TIGO or Kasapa™ cell phone while in Ghana or purchase minutes to 'top up' a borrowed cell phone owned by a trusted Ghanaian.

Entry Requirements: A passport and visa are required, as is evidence of a yellow fever vaccination. (Pregnant women and documented medical exemptions are the only exceptions). Travelers should obtain the latest information details from:

> **Embassy of Ghana**
> The Consular Section
> 3512 International Drive, NW,
> Washington, DC 20008 USA
> Telephone (202) 686-4520
>
> **U.S. Ambassador Donald G. Teitelbaum**
> Embassy: 24 4th Circular Road
> Cantonments, Accra Ghana
> Mailing address: P. O. Box 194, Accra
> Telephone: [233] 21.741-000 FAX: [233] 21. 741-389

Basic Documentation

Keep a list and photo copies of the following documents at home with a trusted person you can contact in case of emergency. Check off each as you collect them.

- A copy of your passport and visa pages
- A copy of your airline ticket, so that person can call the ticket issuer in the U. S., for you if yours is lost
- A schedule of your itinerary and how to get in touch with you
- A copy of your special health conditions, medical inoculations and insurance information
- Power of Attorney so your spouse or caretaker of minor children, may be authorized for emergency or medical procedures

Also carry the following:

- ⌗ An extra set of passport / visa photos, in case you visit another country
- ⌗ Your Driver's License
- ⌗ Certificate of Vaccination
- ⌗ Basic First Aid Kit
- ⌗ Cameras and extra film, memory cards etc.

NOTE: Taking pictures in airports, military sites, government buildings, is **Prohibited.**

- ⌗ Rechargeable or spare batteries for electronics. The local electrical current is 220V. Buy a Voltage regulator or step-up/ step-down when you arrive
- ⌗ Wear a concealed money pouch for valuables
- ⌗ Spare set of luggage keys
- ⌗ Aquatic beach shoes for the rocky seashores
- ⌗ Portable water bottle in a carrying case w/ shoulder strap
- ⌗ Pocket flashlight (for the occasional power shortages. You can buy candles once you arrive and small boxed matches)
- ⌗ Hand sanitizer and wet wipes
- ⌗ Business cards or stickers with your email address just for GH contacts
- ⌗ A 3 day supply of packaged dried fruit 'n snacks.

TIP: Once you discover the delicious, natural, groundnuts (peanuts), cashews, almonds, biscuits (cookies), Fango™ frozen desserts, kelli-welli—deep fried, wonderfully delicious, plantain chunks (sold only at night) and the nearest imported goodies at your neighborhood Gas Station—you'll think you are at a 'Starvin Marvin's', 7-Eleven, Pilots, etc. Tourists and nationals hang out at these Bar 'n Grill stations for a night of music and entertainment. Check out the goodies yourself.

FOR YOUR HEALTH

Information on vaccinations and other health precautions may be obtained from the Centers for Disease Control Prevention's, international traveler's Hotline phone 1-877-FYI-TRIP (1-877-394-8787), FAX 1-888-CDC-FAXX (1-888-232-3299) or visit CDC Internet home page at http://www.cdc.gov.

H20
Drink only bottled water or small purified bagged Nsu/water. Imported favorites can be found too. As soon as you arrive purchase in bulk a case of 1.5 L bottled water. It's very inexpensive, safe, and you'll consume all with no problem. Voltic® is the water of choice; because it comes from the sweet Volta Region.

G6PD Test
Before taking any new medicines or inoculations for travel, have a physical examination. Specifically ask for a G6PD Blood sugar test. Some people of color cannot take malaria derivatives and must seek natural, alternative medicine.
Read **iTALWAY™ HANDBOOK: Medicine Plants and Home Remedies by D. N. A**.

RX
Bring a (30) day supply of any medications, and a spare pair of eye glasses.

Medical Facilities

Medical facilities are limited, particularly outside Accra. Doctors and hospitals accept Cash Only payments for health care services. If given a 'Drip' (an I.V.) or any 'drugs' (medications), all will all be added to your Final Bill. **NOTE**: Personal toiletries are not provided for overnight stays. Your foreign medical insurance, Medicare/Medicaid will not be accepted for treatment. Consult your own insurance provider regarding overseas treatment; including medical evacuation. Ascertain whether you will be reimbursed for any expenses.

Mosquito Bites

Avoid scratching the bite. Rub any liquid soap on the area to relieve itching or Witch Hazel. Splash freshly squeezed lemon/lime juice on your skin after bathing; then it is safer to go out early dawn or after sunset. Minimize the use of perfumes. If you're not so sweet tasting the mosquitoes won't bite. Read **iTALWAY™ HANDBOOK: Medicine Plants and Home Remedies** by D. N. A. for additional protection.

Diet

Most importantly, you must realize that you're visiting a region, season and climate, significantly different from your point of departure. Ghana, West Africa, is approximately 11° North of the Equator and 4° East of the Prime Meridian. During your first 24 hours, it is recommended that you do not jump heavy into anything. Only dine on fruits and bottled water the first day. Enjoy a few sites by motoring then chill by the pool. Simply put, your metabolism needs time to adjust; so, for the first day move slowly and re-hydrate. (*It is not uncommon that after a few days or one week of being here, that diarrhea or malaria can attack—be prepared.

The following days, you can "shop 'til you drop" and treat yourself to some of Ghana's fine cuisine. Such as, Kontumbre Stew (high in iron and calcium) prepared with agushie sauce and yam. Kontumbre is a green leafy vegetable used in many dishes. Ghana also has wild Jamaican Calaloo; eat plenty and enjoy it in a variety of ways, including steamed with coconut cream. Jollof Rice, similar to Spanish rice, is a tasty mixture of fried rice and vegetables, prepared with a unique blend of seasonings to enhance the flavor. By all means you must try the national favorites, eaten solely with fingers: banku, kenkey and fufu. One of my favorites, sold only at night are keleweles, chunks of ripe plantain fried with yummy spices. MMmmm Good!

Ghana has been richly blessed by the Creator with an abundance of coconuts (koo-bay). These electrolyzed, sweet potassium filled fruits are a 'must have'. I truly feel that they serve a major part in keeping healthy and 'dis-ease' free.

Remember: "A Koo-bay a day, keeps the doctor away" and your immune system will thank you. I reside in mango and pineapple paradise year round. Enjoy foods with the highest forms of nutrition.

Luggage

For international destinations you are permitted two (*2) checked pieces of luggage each no more than 50 lb. each. (* Subject to change) Airlines may charge $150-$300 for each extra bag. After CUSTOMS has inspected the contents of your luggage, wise travelers combine two pieces of luggage with self-sealing 'Saran Wrap', to create one checked item. For example, wrap a duffel bag with a small box to be checked in as a single piece. Then do the same for the second piece. You are entitled two (2) carry-on items, not exceeding 12lb each and size is strictly enforced. NOTE: A purses and pocketbooks are considered carry-on. Temporarily stuff it into the larger carry-on. The airline agents will be counting and they might weigh and measure these! Travel light so that you can return with plenty of items from the Motherland. If possible, nest one med-size empty suitcase inside a larger one before you start packing. On the return trip home you'll have a 2nd suitcase—which is easily filled.

Don't return to the states with all the stuff you took. Trade as many items for things you'd like; thereby, creating more space in your luggage for all your new purchases. Ghana has a plethora of highly skilled and gifted seamstresses and tailors that can design and make garments to your specifications. **Suggestion:** Be sure to have your new garments embroidered. The small price you'll pay for Batik and Kente cloth are "sweeto", so you can buy "plentyo".

SECURITY

Security is an essential part of advance planning for a pleasant journey. Pick-pocketing, purse snatching, and various types of scams are the common forms of crime confronting visitors. Avoid the excessive display real 'bling-blings' in public and flashing large rolls of cash. Be discreet and humble. If you didn't do dumb stuff back home, don't start now. However, if you are the victim of any crime, file a local **Police Report and call 191** (don't expect officers to come to the crime scene unless you pick them up.) Americans should also notify the:

USA Regional Security Office 021.741-5500

Money Matters

Notify your credit/charge/debt card companies that you intend to travel abroad, they will advise you of their policies and international surcharges. Wear a concealed money pouch or neck pouch to hold your U.S. passport and U.S. money. Bulging pockets and large purses are discouraged. Once you settle into your lodgings, convert $100-$200 to the local currency New Ghana Cedis (¢). One U. S. Dollar = GH¢1.35* (GH¢1 Cedi + 35 pesewas) at an authorized FOREX (Foreign Exchange) Bureau and/or ECO, Stanbic, Barclays Bank. *Exchange rates are subject to change.

The new Ghana Cedi Notes are:
Red GH ¢1 One Cedi
Blue GH ¢5 Five Cedis
Green GH ¢10 Ten Cedis
Purple GH ¢ 20 Twenty Cedis
Brown GH ¢ 50 Fifty Cedis

The new Ghana coins are:
Copper 1 pesewa represents the Akosombo Dam
Silver 5 pesewas represents the music
Silver 10 pesewas represents the Universities
Silver 20 pesewas represents Cocoa
Silver 50 pesewas represents the Market Women
Silver and Gold coin is 1 Cedi equivalent to 100
pesewas and represents the Courts.

Bartering, Gifts and Dashing

You'll be surprised how quickly your US dollars will disappear, but you'll still have bargaining power with trade items such as;

Trendy flashlights
Batteries
Small trendy transistor radios
Music CDs
New T-shirts with logos
Baseball caps
Hair ornaments
Sunglasses
U. S. recorded music
Tech and hobby magazines
Fashion magazines featuring people of color

> Cologne
> Dusting powder
> Portable water bottles (freebies from various companies)
> Sticky note pads (bright colors)
> Ink pens, pencils, felt markers,
> Individually wrapped candy

Upon arriving at Kotoka International Airport, select one Porter/Sky cap and pay him $5 US for 2-3 pieces of luggage, if assistance is needed. Free trolley carts are available at the baggage claim area and may be pushed all the way outdoors.

A simple rule of thumb after calculating a tip/dash for good service, personally hand the individuals their dash / tip. Place it directly into their right hand, instead of adding it to your credit card. Automatically adding gratuities to your bill does not always work to the benefit of your server or chamber maid.

Tip / dash your tour guide daily and feed them whenever you eat. They may prefer a daily monetary dash, which would cover their transportation to and from work. Some tour groups take up a collection before their last day and present the guide with a love gift. [Personal gifts are appropriate too.]

For general helpful, courteous, public services, dash GH ¢1.

NOTE: On the street bartering is debatable because you'll be bombarded with a mass of people—use discretion.

Traffic Safety and Transportation

You will encounter road conditions that differ significantly from those in the U. S. The primary roads are paved and well maintained. However, the roads from Accra to the Central Region's tourist attractions in Cape Coast, continues to be the site of many highway accidents. The unpredictable behavior of pedestrians, cyclist, and farm animals, such as sheep, goats, and longhorns can be dangerous. Driving after sunset, particularly on rural roads, is extremely hazardous, due to no or poor street lighting. ALL road signs are in **kilometers**; please convert the speed and do not put the 'pedal to the metal. You might see the Police clocking you with a Radar Detector. Always have your ID and auto documents available to present at the numerous Check Points.

The circle-about intersections are unfamiliar to most North Americans and might prove challenging; fortunately, Ghanaians drive on the same side of the road as Americans. Your state Driver's License from home is acceptable for short visits. However, long term residents must acquire a Ghana license—it's the size of a miniature passport book. Vehicles can be rented at better hotels and various sites in Accra. Many people prefer to **Charter** (hire) a private taxi driver for a day(s). Or request a taxi to take you directly to a location called a **Drop,** prices are negotiable. **Local taxis** have fixed routes, fixed prices and will be shared by other people along the route. Eventually, you will learn the various hand signals to summon the correct vehicle; such as a series of circles with the entire hand; pointing up; pointing down; or, just plain old waving all fingers up and down. Have fun!

An economical alternative for long journeys are the **S.T.C.** buses, operated by the **S**tate **T**ransit **C**ompany. They provide very upscale, comfortable and sometimes air-conditioned motor coaches to each region.

NOTE: Schedules are **S**ubject **T**o **C**hange (STC), so enjoy your snacks, music, companions or a good book while waiting.

It is even less costly to squeeze into a 12 passenger van/'tro-tro' with 16 people toting: chickens in a basket, auto parts, fresh fish, luggage . . .

Be adventurous and board an inter-city Metro Bus. It makes local stops throughout Accra and other regions. School children in uniform ride FREE. Look for the BIG, bright, orange colored, bus and buy your ticket at the little orange booth.

Or, avoid long road journeys and travel by commercial domestic aircrafts to Kumasi, Tamale, Takoradi and other distant regions. Check with a reliable Travel Agent.

CULTURAL ETIQUETTE

Ghana's official language is English, but it's the Queen's English, which has spellings and pronunciations quite different from the American English. When in doubt ask questions or consult and International Dictionary. Be willing to learn a few expressions in one of the native tongues. Everyone will smile in appreciation that you are making an effort; no matter how strange you sound. [Refer to the LANGUAGE Section]

Patience, *patience please*
As our Ghanaian brothers and sisters will tell you "wait small, small." A scheduled event or meeting rarely starts on time; so remember, C.P. time is here too. Our beautiful kinsmen will get the job done; but not at the fast, zoom-zoom pace to which you are accustomed. They may even engage the assistance of their comrade(s) to keep from disappointing you—but the mission will be accomplished.

In the event that you are graced by an audience with a traditional Chief, ladies, please do not wear shorts and mini-skirts. Wear a longer, calf length skirt. When seated, legs, ankles and knees must be Uncrossed. Everyone must remain silent, until permission is granted. No photos

Upon visiting someone's home you will be offered water/Nsu, politely reply "thank you, I am fine." It's customary for you to bring drinks—sodas, sack of water pouches, spirit water, etc. for a host or of Chief/Nana. Ask your guide for details.

If you want to go to the lavatory, ask for the TOILET, otherwise, you might be directed to the roadside urinal.

P.S. <u>Always</u> carry toilet tissue and strike a match to kill the odor in the public KV. Your hand sanitizer will be very useful too.

Try not to stare too long at Mothers breast feeding their blessed child. These are healthy, natural occurrences in the city, village and on the Tro-tro.

Also, close your dropped jaw when you see people urinating/**p**issing **i**n **p**ublic ("P.I.P.") It happens frequently when nature calls, but facilities are few.

Pen Pals

Many adults and children want to be your new friend, and come to America; so, you will be asked to assist them. Be firm and honest with your decision. Bring pre-printed address from USA youth, organizations and individuals if you are willing to be the postmaster.

Be prepared to be addressed as: Aunty, Uncle, Sister, Brother, Mama, Daddy, or Nana; these are words of endearment which makes you part of the Ghanaian family.

Offenses

If you are a person of color, and someone calls you "/o-brew-nee/," STOP the conversation and inform them your ancestors were African and you are not Caucasian.

Now, for all you left handed people like myself, you better start to practice eating, waving, receiving and giving items with only the right hand, (even though the left hand is clean because it helped wash the right) it is a taboo.

The hand gesture O.K. signaled by a circle and three raised fingers; and, the raised thumbs up, are both non-verbal insults.

If you are a houseguest, offer to purchase minerals (sodas) and food for the household. Your host would NEVER ask for 1 pesewa = 1 penny. Demonstrate your appreciation before your departure. Your initial visit was made comfortable at great expense, just like we do when company is expected, we royal out the royal carpet.

When it is time for a bath, but the pipe water is not flowing, your host will provide a large, fresh bucket of water and a smaller pail for communal purpose. Try not to use all the water for yourself or discard soapy water into the clean pail, since other people will also share the same clean water. Water shortages can occur anytime.

Whenever laundry services are needed, a wash person will be hired to hand laundry your clothes. Offer them a cool drink and something to eat and watch this process—it's a lot of work! They will hang your clothes on a dry-line and professionally iron them. You will surely miss this special service when you return to the states. Ask the hostess how much to pay the individual.

Photography
Taking pictures in airports, military sites, government buildings, is **prohibited.**

Always ask, "May I take your picture?" If they want payment . . . that is your cue to leave, others may wave, signaling NO.

Most Ghanaians will love to have their pictures taken; so, bring inexpensive or disposable cameras, these are popular commodities to barter and they make great gifts. Keep your word if copies of the photographed person are promised.

When your camera memory is full, you can off-load it at Busy Internet or any fast public Internet Café. They can accommodate your laptop too.

CLOTHING

Ghana is in the tropics and it is always *Hot—Medium Hot,* with two rainy seasons, April—June and September—November. Therefore, natural fibers, loose fit clothing and cotton undergarments are advised. Purchase sun caps and straw hats once you deplane.

The wearing of any military apparel, such as army fatigues, camouflage jackets, trousers or any clothing items which may appear military in nature are **Strongly Discouraged.**

Mini-skirts, short shorts, and 'Hoochie Mama' clothing are not advised for adult females. Unfortunately, the young boys wear 'sagging pants' here too!

Do you remember why Grandma or Big Mama always carried a handkerchief? Well, I do. The heat of these tropical days will cause your body to glisten profusely (as females do); or perspire (as men do). Sticky, wet clothing cannot be avoided; at least, your face can appear dry and cool. The artisans make fabulous fans. Hint: Start your own collection.

Believe me, you will want to leave your cute, thin sole, Italian made shoes at home! The roads will eat and tear them up 'plentyo'. Go a U.S. shoe outlet/warehouse and buy a pair of thick rubber sole sandals with straps, and an enclosed walking shoe / gym shoe. (Before you depart Ghana, dash them to someone or barter.) Once you arrive, purchase some locally handmade footwear from the talented artisans. I bought a beautiful pair of sandals made of corn husks and recycled tires for the soles. You will be culturally and ecologically correct, look good and supportive of the nation's economy. Flip-flops are available at any outdoor market.

SHOPPING

AKWAABA—WELCOME TO GREATER ACCRA where you can "shop til you drop." You while probably run out of time or Cedis before running out of great stores and markets for bargains. If you like air conditioned venues, there are a couple malls near the Kotoka International Airport. You can purchase everything from gold to tennis balls, or fine imported wine and cheese.

- The Accra Mall @ Tetteh Quashie Roundabout
- A & C Shopping Mall @ East Legon

Discover your greatest bargains at the arts and craft centres or open markets. These dealers will negotiate prices with you; remember, the better your skills the lower the price.

As you tour other regions more beauties await you: baskets, beads, clothing, woodcarvings, paintings, and jewelry. Yes, gold, diamonds copper, and silver are mined in Ghana.

TOURING

Extensive tourist information is available in most regions (for sale) at the **Ghana Tourist Board.** The Greater Accra head office is near the Novotel Hotel. While in the Capital—

Greater Accra Region GR visit:
- Kwame Nkrumah Mausoleum and Museum
- Centre for National Culture B.K.A. "Arts Centre"
- Accra International Conference Centre
- National Theatre
- National Museum
- Osu Castle (the Presidential Office
- W.E.B. DuBois Memorial Center for Pan Afrikan Culture
- University of Ghana—Legon
- Makola Market
- Kaneshie Open Market
- Tema
- Accra Zoo

Central Region CR visit:
- See any of the 76 Slave Forts/dungeons along the Gold Coast. Astute guides are available at the Cape Coast and Elmina Dungeons. *Avoid non-melanin tag-a-longs during this revered event.
- University of Cape Coast
- Elimina Harbor
- Kakum National Park *Wear enclosed shoes and keep your hands free to grasp the canopy rope in the tree tops.

- University of Ghana—Winneba
- Winneba fishing villages for pottery and ceramics

Ashanti Region GA visit:
- Lake Bosumtwi
- Owabi Bird Sanctuary
- Bomfobiri Wildlife Sancturay
- Bonwire Village 'Kente weaving'
- Kumasi Market
- Obuasi Ashanti Goldfields *Appointment required
- Ntonso (home of Adrinkra cloth)

Brong Ahafo Region
- Bia National Park
- Boabeng-Fiema Wildlife Sanctuary
- Fuller Falls
- Digya National Park

Eastern Region GE visit:
- Aburi Botanical Gardens
- Akosombo Lake and Dam
- Boti Falls (June and August)
- Koforidua (Thursday morning Bead Market)

Northern Region visit:
- Larabanga (oldest mosques in West Africa)
- Mole National Park

Upper East Region visit:
- Bolgatanga (traditional clothing, baskets, and leather goods from Mali and Burkina Faso traders every 3rd day)

- Paga Crocodile Pond

Upper West Region visit:
- Wa (traditional Sudanese style mosque)

Volta Region GV visit:
- Lake Volta
- Bui Waterfalls
- Kalakpe Game Reserve
- The Caves of Nyagbo and Logba
- Kyabobo National Park
- Atorkor Slave Fort
- Agbozume Kente weaving village
- Amedzofe mountain climbing
- Hohoe
- Wli Falls

Western Region GW visit:
- Takoradi
- Tarkwa Gold Mine *An appointment maybe required
- Nsuta Manganese Mine
- Dr. Nkrumah's original grave
- Forts / Slave dungeons
- Nzulezo Stilt Village

LODGINGS *Based on 2009 rates

Labadi Beach Hotel Phone: 021772501 Average price*: **$324**

La Palm Royal Beach Hotel Phone: 021771700 Average price* **$280**

Golden Tulip Hotel Accra Phone: 021775360 Average price*: **$277**

Novotel Hotel Accra City Centre Phone: 021667546 Average price*:**$191**

Holiday Inn Accra Airport Phone: 021 Average price*: **$314**

Hotel Shangri-La Phone: 021776993 Average price*: **$150**

African Royal Beach Hotel Phone: Average price*: **$171**

Dutch Hotel Nshonaa Phone: 0217111 Average price*: **$55**

Coconut Grove Regency Hotel Accra Phone: 021225155 Average price*: **$**

The above *HOTELS* offer internet and/or wireless service

Hotel Chez-Moi Phone: 021512949 Average price*: **$40**

Hotel Hansonic Phone: Average price*: **$19**

Stone Lodge Greater Accra Phone: Average price*: **$45**

Coconut Grove Beach Resort, Elmina Central Region Phone: 04291213

Elmina Beach Resort, Elmina Phone: 04233743 Average price*: **$40**

Fairhill Guesthouses, Cape Coast Phone: 04233322 Average price*: **$40**

Mable's Tables and Guest House, Phone: 0244610009 Average price*: **$30**

Saana Lodge Phone:

Anomabu Beach Resort Phone: 04233801

Biriwa Beach Phone: 04233333

Axim Beach Hotel Phone:

Busua Beach Resort Phone:

Rainbow Garden Village Guesthouse Phone: Average price*: **$55**

Golden Tulip Hotel Kumasi City Phone: Average price*: **$184**

*Additional modest priced lodgings are available with **Guest Houses,** which are similar to Bed & Breakfast facilities. Also, the universities have real nice chalets and guest lodgings for rent.

BUSINESS VENTURES

". . . Ghana has emerged as "Black Africa's Economic Showcase . . . Ghana's people have proved themselves to be resilient and worthy of future success." [Ghana 40th Anniversary, 1997, p. 15.] An environment of investment opportunities awaits you and Ghana is ready for business!

However, if you're looking for free land—FORGET IT, anything of value has a price. Please avoid any secret business deals with your 'new friends'. Seek advice of an Ababio (Repatriated Diasporan i.e. a person of African descent born as a direct result of the African Holocaust) living in that area. Ghana needs serious, conscientious entrepreneurs with cash and materials. Do your homework and speak to the Chief; pay for a land survey and title search, then register the deed in Accra; next, follow-up with multiple, return visits. Take photographs of your new venture, partners, and get detailed receipts.

The Government of Ghana maintains strict regulations involving transactions of natural resources, i.e., gold, diamonds and precious metals. All legitimate agents must be licensed and all transactions must be certified. The Government requires all business ventures established by internationals to have a Ghanaian business partner. This 'buddy system' helps foreigners learn how to comport themselves in a new environment and insures that future revenues include Ghanaians.

LANGUAGE

The National Language in Ghana is English, however, the people are multi-lingual. The main languages are Fante, Twi and GA. Visit your Main Library's Language Department, it has an extensive inventory of foreign languages, which include books and read-along learning tapes. You can learn conversational expressions while on your way to work, or during leisure time via a Walkman, iPod, etc. Since cassette tapes are mobile, it's very useful, even without the read-along book. Unfortunately, most libraries have not acquired language tapes for Ghana's multitude of languages: Ewe, Fante, Twi, Ga, Hausa, Ashanti. Visit your local Pan African Centre, Department of African History at universities; or, an African Centered School/Academy; because, they can direct you to the local Ghanaian communities for real conversation. If possible, purchase a current edition of the <u>Ghana Travel Guide,</u> it is very detailed and accurate. In lieu of audio recordings, selected Ghanaian phrases and dialect information has been compiled for your benefit.

FANTE ALPHABET
(Mfantse Akyerɛwamba)

UPPERCASE

A	B	D	E	Ɛ	F	G
H	I	K	(L)	M	N	O
Ɔ	P	R	S	T	U	W
Y	(Z)					

*(L) Must be in front of borrowed words eg. Lɔɔre—/Lorry/

*(Z) Cannot stand alone. Add 'd' eg. Dzi—to eat; dzin—strong

MFANTSE AKYEREWAMBA SOUNDS

A	-	ah	
B	-	b	/boot/
D	-	du	/duck/
E	-	ē	*high tone
Ɛ	-		/egg/
F	-		/fat/
G	-		/get/
H	-		/hay/
I	-	ee	/ill/
			*low tone
K	-		/cut/
L	-	ēl	
M	-	mm	
N	-	nn	
O	-	ō	
Ɔ	-		/all/
P	-		/pop/
R	-	rr	
S	-	ss	/sing/
T	-		*short sound
U	-	ö	/cool/
W	-		/way/
Y	-		/yes/
Z	-	zed	/zero/

FANTE Continued

WIDE VOWELS

a	ɛ	e	ɔ	o
/father/	/best/	/pit/	/pot/	/put/
ba	yɛ	se	sɔ	fow
to come;	to do;	to say;	to taste;	to climb

NOTE: The vowels 'e' and 'o' each have multiple sounds.

Narrow Vowels (Nasal Sound)

e	i	o	u
/fate/	/fee/	/so/	/two/
ye	fi	dondo	tu
to be good	to go away	a drum	to fly

MFANTSE Consonants

The MFANTSE consonants are the same as in English except: **c, j, q, v,** and **x** are not used.

Diagraphs are two letter combinations

dw	dz	gy	hw	hy
/jewel/	/zebra/	/judge/	/what/	/shirt/
dwɛɛtee	dzin	gya	hwen	hyɛ
money;	name;	to receive;	nose	to wear

kw	ky	ny	tw
/quack/	/church/	/canyon/	/choose/
kwan	kyɛw	nyansa	twuw
road;	hat;	wisdom	to grate

MFANTSE BIRTH NAMES

FEMALE	MALE	
Esi	Kwesi	Sunday born
Adwowa	Kodwo	Monday
Abena	Kwabena	Tuesday
Ekua	Kwaku	Wednesday
Yaa	Yaw	Thursday
Efua	Kofi	Friday
Ama	Kwame	Saturday

GREETINGS AND RESPONSES/NKYIA NA NGYEDO

Good morning	Mema wo akye; maakye
Good afternoon	Mema wo aha; maaha
Good evening	Mema wo adwe
Goodnight	Ma adze nkye
Welcome	Da yie / Akwaaba
I welcome you	Mema wo akɔaba
How are you?	W'apɔw mu ɛ?
	Wo honam mu ɛ?
	Wo ho ta den?

FANTE CONTINUED

I am fine	Mo ho ye
	Bokɔ
How is your wife and children?	Wo yer ma wo mba ho tse dɛn?
They are all fine	Hɔn ho ye
I am pleased to meet you	Yeehyiahyia oo!
Greeting a Chief	Yaa Nana
Greeting an elder man	Yaa egya
Greeting a mother	Yaa na
Greeting a worker/ Laborer	Aeyko?
Goodbye	Bye

EƲE / EWE LANGUAGE

Pronounced: **/eh-veh/**

Eʋe is spoken in the Volta Region of Ghana, Benin, Togo, Nigeria and by nationals residing in the diaspora. The coastal Eʋes, being mostly traders and fishermen, are found in almost every town in Ghana.

Eʋe is a tonal language and changes in meaning can be brought about by tonal differences. It has a number of peculiar consonants and digraphs. It is hoped that this small introduction can help you to learn Eʋe with minimal difficulty.

[Adapted: Language Guide—Ewe Version, Bureau of Ghana Languages, Third Edition 1997]

EƲE / EWE ALPHABET

Aa	Bb	Dd	Ɖɖ	Ee	Ɛɛ	Ff	Ƒƒ	Gg
Ɣɣ	Hh	Xx	Ii	Kk	Ll	Mm	Nn	Ŋŋ
Oo	Ɔɔ	Pp	Rr	Ss	Tt	Uu	Vv	Ʋʋ
Ww	Yy	Zz						

EWE ALPHABET SOUNDS

A - /cast/

B - /be/

D - /de/ high sound

Đ - /de/ low sound

E - /eight/

Ɛ - /egg/ nasal

F - /fufu/

Ƒ - /pair/

G - /gut/

Ɣ - /him/

H - /her/

X - /hook/ voiceless

I - /feet/

K - /cup/

L - /leg/

M - /mm/

N - /no/ high sound

Ŋ - /ing/ like sing

O - /goal/

Ɔ - /cost/

P - /per/

R - /r-rest/

S - /sit/

T - /term/

U - /cool/

V - /vulture/

Ʋ - a voiced 'f'

W - /way/

Y - /yawn/

Z - /zebra

EWE VOWEL SOUNDS

There are seven (7) significant vowels in Eʋe: a, e, ɛ, i, ɔ, o, u

a sounds like	a in cast
e sounds like	ei in eight
ɛ sounds like	e in egg
i sounds like	ee in feet
ɔ sounds like	o in cost
o sounds like	o in goal
u sounds like	oo in cool

CONSONANT SOUNDS

There are 23 consonants. These include all the English consonants except C, J and Q.

Six of them are not in English: Ðɖ, Ƒf, Ɣɣ, Xx, Ŋŋ, Vʋ.

Ðɖ   is softer and is pronounced slightly farther back than the English 'd'

Ƒf   is a bilabial f; pronounced with both lips, as if you were blowing out a candle

Ɣɣ   is produced as a soft guttural sound, like a very soft 'h'

Xx   is voiceless, pronounced like a voiceless 'h'

Ŋŋ   is pronounced like 'ng' in sing

Uʊ　　is a voiced f. It sounds like the English "v' pronounced with both lips.

The remaining consonants are pronounced as English sounds.

EUE DIAGRAPHS

The diagraphs that foreigners find difficult to pronounce are: ts, tsy, dz, kp, gb and ny.

Ts　　sounds like　　ts in hits　　eg. Tsi—water

Tsy　　sounds like　　ch in chair　　eg. Tsɔysyɔ—dark

Dz　　sounds like　　ts, but it is noticeably softer and voiced
　　　　　　　　　　eg. Dze—salt

Kp　　position the tongue as for k, the lips for p, and then release the two, closing simultaneously.
　　　　　　　　　　eg. Kpe—stone

Gb　　sounds　　like kp, but it is softer, voiced and heavier
　　　　　　　　　　eg. Gbe—voice

Ny　　sounds like onion　　eg. Nya—word

*Please note: There are no exact English equivalents for most of these sounds; the examples given are the nearest English comparisons.

Now you can recite the ABC's in EVE!

EWE Continued

NUMBERS XEXLEMEWO

1	Ðeka	15	Wuiatɔ
2	Eve	16	Wuiadre
3	Etɔ	17	Wuienyi
4	Ene	18	Wuiasieke
5	Ato	19	Blaeve
6	Ade	20	Blaeve vɔ ɖeke
7	Adre	30	Blaetɔ
8	Tnyi	40	Blaene
9	Asieke	100	Alafa ɖeka
10	Ewo	200	Alafa eve
11	Wuiɖekɛ	1,000	Akpe ɖeka
12	Wuieve	1,000,000	Miliɔn ɖeka
13	Wuietɔ		
14	Wuiene		

EXPRESSIONS EVE PRONUNCIATION

Please	Mede kuku	/[mehdeh koo.koo/
Thank you	Akpe	/ahk-pay/
	Akpe na wo	/ahk-pay nawoe/
Go	Dzo	/joe/
Come	Va	
Yes	Ee	/aae/
No	Ao	/ow/
I don't understand	Nyemese egɔme o	
		/ny-ma-say—goma o/
Say it again	Gagblɔe	/ga-blay-ah/
Say it slowly	Gblɔe blewuu	
What is your name?	Nkɔ wo de?	
My name is (Adzowa)	Nye Nkɔ e (Adzowa)	
Good morning	Ndi nawo	
Good afternoon	Ndɔ nawo	
Good	evening Fie	
Goodnight	Zame nenyo	
	Dɔ nyme	
Welcome	Woezɔ	/wayzo/
How are you?	Efɔa?	
	Alekee?	
I am fine	Mefɔ	
	Meli	
I am pleased	Enye dzidzo nambe to meet you	

EWE EXPRESSIONS Continued

Greeting a Chief	Tɔgbui,Togbui, Torgbui
How much is . . .	Ho nenie?
How many . . .	Nenie?
I	Nye
You	wo
Me	Nye
He	Eya
She	Eya
We	Mi
It	Eya
They	Wo
Safe journey	Hede nynie, Xede nynie

EWE BIRTH NAMES

DAY	MALE	FEMALE
Sunday/Kwasida	Kɔsi, Kwasi	Kɔsi wɔ, Kwasiwa
Monday/Dzoda	Kɔozo, Kudzo	Adzo, Adzowa
Tuesday/Brada	Kɔbla, Kwabla	Abla, Ablewa
Wednesday/Kuda	Kɔku	Akua, Aku, Akuwa
Thursday/Yawoda	Yao	Yawa, Yawo
Friday/Fida	Kofi	Afi, Afua, Fuya
Saturday/Memleda	Kɔmi, Kwami	Ama, Ami

TWI EXPRESSIONS

English	Twi Pronunciation
Welcome	/ak-waa-ba/
Yes	/ine/
No	/da-bee/
How are you?	/et-e-sane/
Good morning	/me-ho-wa-chi/
Good afternoon	/maa-ha/
Good evening	/maaj-wo/
Congratulations	/ay-ekoo/
Come	/bra/
Go	/kaw/
OK	/yo/
Thank you	/ma-da-ce/
Please	/ma-pow-cho/
How much?	/a-hen/
What is your name?	/wo-din-de-sen/
Can I pass or Come in?	/ah-go/?

Chuckle and SMILE

There will be so many expressions / scenes that will make you smile. These are just a few that still make me go . . .

HA—HA	TRANSLATION
Rubber	Refers to any plastic bag, not a Condom!
I am coming	A person is leaving but will return sooner or later
Wait small	You may wait a BIG amount of time for an appointment or a task to be completed
Highly Inflammable	A truck transporting flammable materials
Tipper	A dump truck
Drip	An intravenous medical procedure a.k.a. I.V.
Drugs	Legally prescribed medicine from a Doctor or Pharmacy
Hawkers	Vendors, on foot, in traffic selling items
It's off	Refers to any spoiled food

Torch	Flashlight
Step Up/Step Down	An electrical transformer box/platform to convert 110 current to 220. The plugging of a 110 appliance is stepped up to 220 current.
Dressed Chicken	The head, feet, feathers and guts have been removed.
Dressed Fish	The scales and guts have been removed. Not necessarily filleted or beheaded. (Supposedly, eating the head makes one smarter)
Dressed bed	A neatly made up the bed.
Dress	A word to identify clothing worn by either sex
Bath costume	Beachwear, swimming suit
Charlie Wote	Rubber 'flip-flops' slippers. For beach, poolside, home or shower. Not worn for business.
Cold House	Commercial deep freezer facility
Ice Blocks	Frozen plastic bags of water
Nsu	Drinking water in a rubber/plastic sachet
Nsu paa	Pure, filtered, drinking water

Pension Scheme & National Health Insurance Scheme

Yes, it's similar to to the insurance SCHEME in the USA

IRS

Yup, Internal Revenue Scheme

Kra-Kra, Pain, Atta

Twins

Attorney, Barrister

A lawyer in court wearing a white wig and a black robe—just like the old movies

Choir dress

A graduation gown plus the cap and tassel

Indispose

Implies the person is sickly or dead

Sweeping dirt

The outdoor sand and dirt will be artistically swept with a short palm broom—daily!

Winning

Illegal removal of sand from the beach/ seashore to be used for construction

'Red'

In reference to ripe food

"I beg"

An earnest request, please

"Sheee"

Shocking response, surprise

Shito, Shitor

Tasty, fresh, black pepper sauce

#!#*!#*#!*#

An expression displeasure, the sound of sucking one's teeth and jaws together

"Shwreh"   You see, I told you so!

"Ssss, Ssss"   Hissing sound to attract someone's attention

The last and my least favorite expression which will be heard frequently is, MASTER! They are not referring to a slave master, just a highly skilled individual, or the title for Mister. Hmmmm!

INTERESTING FACTS TO KNOW BEFORE YOU GO!

[Reference http://www.TheWorld Factbook—Ghana 2009]

Natural resources:
gold, timber, industrial diamonds, bauxite, manganese, fish rubber, cocoa, limestone, salt, petroleum, silver

Terrain:
mostly low plains with dissected plateau in south-central area

Geography note:
Lake Volta is the world's largest artificial lake

Natural hazards:
dry, dusty, Harmatan winds occur from January—March

Population:
23,832,495

Note: estimates take into account the effects of excess mortality due to AIDS; this can result in lower life expectancy, higher infant mortality and death rates, lower population and growth rates in the distribution of population by age and sex than would otherwise be expected

Age structure:
0-14 years: 37.3% (male 4,503,331/female 4,393,104)
15-64 years: 59.1% (male 7,039,696/female 7,042,208)

65 years and over: 3.6% (male 393,364/female 460,792) (2009 est.)

Median age:
total: 20.7 years
male: 20.5 years female: 21 years (2009 est.)

Life expectancy at birth:
total population: 59.85 years
country comparison to the world: 184
male: 58.98 years
female: 60.75 years (2009 est.)

Population growth rate:
1.882% (2009 est.)
country comparison to the world: 67

Birth rate:
28.58 births/1,000 population (2009 est.)
country comparison to the world: 51

Death rate:
9.24 deaths/1,000 population (July 2009 est.)
country comparison to the world: 81

Infant mortality rate:
total: 51.09 deaths/1,000 live births
country comparison to the world: 50
male: 55.32 deaths/1,000 live births
female: 46.74 deaths/1,000 live births (2009 est.)

Total fertility rate:
3.68 children born/woman (2009 est.)
country comparison to the world: 53

Net migration rate:
-0.53 migrant(s)/1,000 population (2009 est.)
country comparison to the world: 114

Urbanization:
urban population: 50% of total population (2008)
rate of urbanization: 3.5% annual rate of change (2005-10 est.)

Sex ratio:
at birth: 1.03 male(s)/female
under 15 years: 1.02 male(s)/female
15-64 years: 1 male(s)/female
65 years and over: 0.85 male(s)/female
total population: 1 male(s)/female (2009 est.)

Ethnic groups:
Akan 45.3%,
Mole-Dagbon 15.2%,
Ewe 11.7%,
Ga-Dangme 7.3%,
Guan 4%,
Gurma 3.6%,
Grusi 2.6%,
Mande-Busanga 1%, other tribes 1.4%, other 7.8% (2000 census)

Religions:

Christian 68.8%
(Pentecostal/Charismatic 24.1%,
Protestant 18.6%,
Catholic 15.1%,
other 11%),
Muslim 15.9%,
traditional 8.5%,
other 0.7%, none 6.1% (2000 census)

Languages:

Asante 14.8%,
Ewe 12.7%,
Fante 9.9%,
Boron (Brong) 4.6%,
Dagomba 4.3%,
Dangme 4.3%,
Dagarte (Dagaba) 3.7%,
Akyem 3.4%,
Ga 3.4%,
Akuapem 2.9%,
other 36.1% (includes English (official)) (2000 census)

Literacy:

definition: age 15 and over can read and write
total population: 57.9%
male: 66.4%
female: 49.8% (2000 census)

Education System:
Crèche / Day Care privately owned
Free Government schools: Primary and Junior Secondary
Senior Secondary partial Government funding
Colleges at cost
Universities at cost

FM Radio Station:
87.9   ATLANTIS
90.5   RADIO GOLD
91.9   VIBE
92.7   Channel R
95.7   GAR
99.7   JOY FM
101.1   TOP RADIO
101.3   BBC
104.3   PEACE FM
105.7   RADIO UNIVERSE

Television
Ghana Television GTV
CNN
CRYSTALTelevision
METRO TV
TV AFRICA
TV3

Satellite television services are also available; as well as cellular phone and internet services.

Look for my next publication:

YOUR ONE WAY TICKET HOME
By D. N. A.

HEY, YOU BETTER KNOW BEFORE YOU GO! is only a small compilation of things that will assist you during your first return to The Motherland. For those who are interested in staying longer and possibly repatriating call: Kohain @ 0244.962202; the W. E. B. Dubois Center 21.776502; or, the African America Association of Accra (AAAA). Make sure you register / notify the U. S. Embassy in Accra of your long-term visit **I.C.E.**

Keep an open mind, relax and enjoy your visit to the **MOTHERLAND!**

AKWAABA

APPENDICES

SLAVE FORTS

Name	Location	Year built	Built by
Ft. Appolonia	Beyin	1756	British
Ft. St. Anthony	Axim	1515	Portuguese
Ft. Groot Friedrichsburg	Prince's Town	1683	Dutch
Ft. Metal Cross	Dixcove	1693	British
Ft. Batenstein	Butri	1650	Swedish
Ft. Orange	Sekondi	1690	Dutch
Ft. St. Sebastian	Shama	1640	Portuguese
Ft. St. Jago	Elmina	1655	Portuguese
Ft. Victoria	Cape Coast	1702	British
Ft. William	Anomabo	1630	Dutch
Ft. Amsterdam	Kromantse	1638	British
Ft. Leydsaamheid	Apam	1698	Dutch
Ft. Good Hope	Senya Bereku	1702	Dutch
Ft. Ussher	Accra	1648	Dutch
Ft. James	Accra	1673	British
Ft. Prinzenstein	Keta	1784	Danish

Source: Ghana Tourist Board 1995

CASTLES

[MISNOMER—royalty never resided here]

Name	Location	Year built	Built by
St. George	Elmina	1482	Portuguese
Caroulsburg	Cape Coast	1653	Swedish
Christianborg	Accra	1659	Danish

Source: Ghana Tourist Board 1995

If you would like to include your favorite notes in the next revision, email DSTRESS2011@yahoo.com

NOTES

NOTES

NOTES

NOTES

NOTES

NOTES

NOTES